To Our "Little Shepherds:"
Rachel + Katina.
With love from
Nana + Grampa
x x x x x   x x x x x
Sept. 2020

Mary
and the
Little Shepherds
of Fatima

by Marlyn Monge, FSP, and Jaymie Stuart Wolfe

illustrated by Maria João Lopes

Pauline
BOOKS & MEDIA
Boston

Library of Congress Control Number: 2016958847

CIP data is available.

ISBN 10: 0-8198-4959-6
ISBN 13: 978-0-8198-4959-5

Published by Pauline Books & Media, 50 Saint Pauls Avenue, Boston, MA 02130–3491

Printed in the U.S.A.

MLSF VSAUSAPEOILL1-2910106 4959-6

www.pauline.org

Pauline Books & Media is the publishing house of the Daughters of St. Paul, an international congregation of women religious serving the Church with the communications media.

2 3 4 5 6 7 8 9   22 21 20 19 18

Lucia dos Santos and her cousins, Francisco and Jacinta Marto, lived in Portugal one hundred years ago. Although they were ordinary children, God chose them to meet the Blessed Virgin Mary and bring her message to the world. This is their extraordinary story.

Francisco, Jacinta, and their nine-year-old cousin Lucia were shepherds. They led the sheep out to pasture every day.

"Can we pray the Rosary the way we usually do?" asked seven-year-old Francisco.

"Sure," said Lucia. "I'll say 'Hail Mary' and you and Jacinta can say 'Holy Mary.'"

"Then we'll have more time to dance while Francisco plays his flute!" added six-year-old Jacinta.

The world was at war, but not much ever happened in the fields outside Fatima. Until one day, an unexpected visitor appeared.

"Don't be afraid. I am the Angel of Peace."

Although they could all see the angel, only Lucia and Jacinta could hear him.

"Pray with me," the angel continued. He bowed down until his shining face touched the ground.

The shepherds did the same. They repeated the angel's words three times.

"Pray often," the angel said. "The hearts of Jesus and Mary are listening to you." Then he left them.

"Don't tell anyone about this," Lucia warned her cousins. "No one would believe us, and we'll get in trouble."

"We won't," Francisco and Jacinta promised.

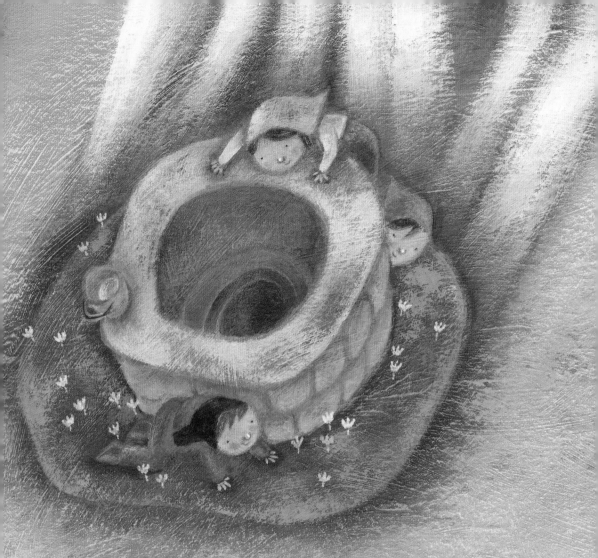

Later in the summer, the angel returned.

"Pray for peace and make sacrifices," he reminded the children.

"How do we make sacrifices?" Lucia asked.

"When you give something up or do something extra because you love God, it is a sacrifice," the angel explained. "If you do this, the war will end. I am your country's guardian, the Angel of Portugal."

From that day on the children looked for ways to make sacrifices.

In September, the angel appeared holding a Chalice and Host.

Leaving the Body and Blood of Christ floating in the air, the angel and the children bowed down in adoration. He then gave the Host to Lucia and offered the Chalice to Jacinta and Francisco.

"Will we see the angel again?" Jacinta asked with a sigh.

None of them knew. Neither could they imagine the even more extraordinary things that would happen.

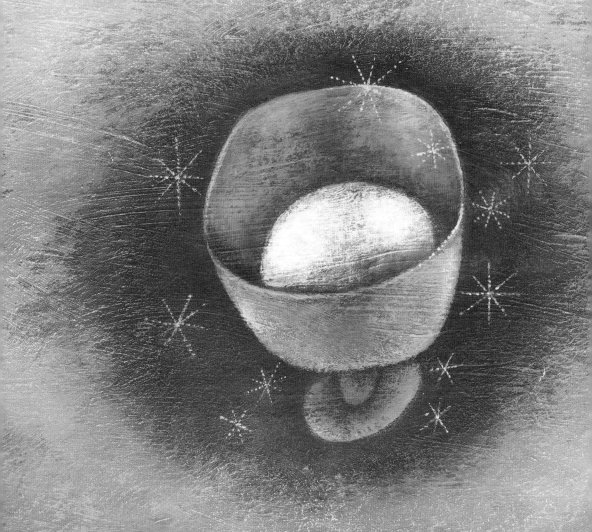

"Let's go to the Cova da Iria," suggested Francisco on May 13, 1917.

Once there, the sheep began to graze. Suddenly, a bright light flashed across the sky. "We'd better go home before the thunderstorm comes!" Lucia exclaimed.

As they were leaving, the children saw a woman dressed in white above a small tree. They were startled.

"Don't be afraid," said the beautiful lady. "I would never hurt you."

"Where are you from? And what do you want?" Lucia asked in awe.

The lady smiled, "I am from heaven. I want you to return on the thirteenth day of the next six months."

"Will we go to heaven?" Lucia wondered aloud.

"You will all go to heaven, but Francisco needs to pray many Rosaries," the lady assured them. "Will you continue to make sacrifices to God so that sinners will turn back to him?

"Yes," Lucia responded for all three of them.

Then the lady went up and up into the blue sky, until she disappeared.

"The lady from heaven was so beautiful!" Jacinta exclaimed.

"Remember, the lady is our secret. You can't tell anyone about her," Lucia said sternly.

"I won't tell anyone," Jacinta promised. "But she was so beautiful!"

Jacinta couldn't seem to talk about anything else all the way home.

Francisco and Lucia grew worried.

That night Jacinta could not keep quiet. "Mama!" she cried out. "A lady from heaven came to us today! She was so beautiful!"

"From heaven? You mean the Blessed Mother?" their mother questioned.

Francisco stared at Jacinta in disbelief.

The next day Francisco told Lucia what had happened.

"I knew you wouldn't be able to keep our secret," Lucia said.

"I couldn't help myself," Jacinta replied with tears in her eyes.

"Don't cry," Lucia whispered, taking her by the hand. "Just don't tell anyone else."

Jacinta never repeated the secret, but her mother told her neighbors. Soon, everyone in Fatima was talking about Jacinta's story. But not everyone believed it. Even Lucia's mother thought her daughter was lying.

The little shepherds returned to the Cova da Iria on June 13, just as Our Lady had asked. Many other people joined them to see if what they had heard was true.

After praying the Rosary, the children saw a flash of light. The Virgin Mary appeared, once again, above the tree.

Jacinta watched and listened. Francisco saw the Lady, but still could not hear her. And Lucia spoke for all of them.

The other people there did not see the flash of light. None of them could see or hear the Lady, nor could they hear what Lucia said.

In between visits from the beautiful lady, the children continued to care for the sheep.

"Francisco, where are you?" Lucia called.

"I'm here! Look up!" Francisco's voice answered. The girls saw his arm waving from higher up the hillside.

"Stay there, we'll come too," Jacinta shouted.

"I'm praying," Francisco responded.

"But we were going to pray the Rosary together," Lucia reminded him.

"I'll still pray with you. But everyone's sins make Jesus so sad," he explained, "I want to tell him how much I love him."

Each of the children tried to do what Our Lady had asked of them. They were always ready to pray and constantly looked for ways to make small sacrifices. None of them could have imagined the difficult days ahead.

Our Lady returned in July and news of the apparitions spread. Even more people came to Fatima to see what was happening. But local officials weren't happy. In August they kept the children from meeting Our Lady at the Cova da Iria.

"I'm taking you where all liars belong—jail!" Mayor Arturo said sharply.

"But we aren't lying!" Jacinta said.

"You may have fooled half of Portugal, but I'm putting an end to this foolishness," he warned.

At his office the mayor questioned the children one at a time. He promised them gifts and threatened them harm. Since the children refused to deny what they had seen, he put them in jail.

Jacinta looked out of the jail cell window. "Mayor Arturo said they're going to kill us for lying," she sobbed. "And we never said goodbye to Mama and Papa."

"I know," said Francisco, hugging his little sister. "But even if we die here, we'll go to heaven."

"Let's pray the Rosary," Lucia suggested.

The children knelt down and soon the other prisoners prayed with them.

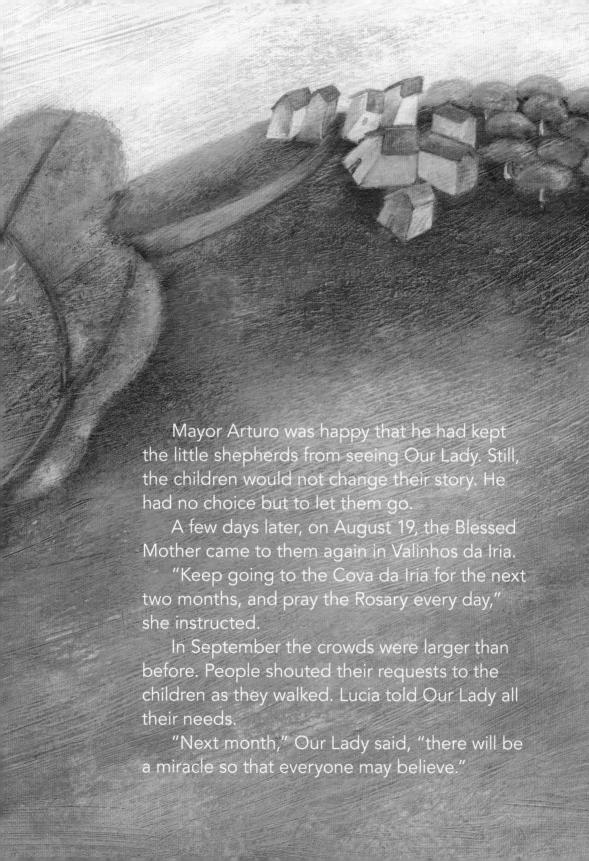

Mayor Arturo was happy that he had kept the little shepherds from seeing Our Lady. Still, the children would not change their story. He had no choice but to let them go.

A few days later, on August 19, the Blessed Mother came to them again in Valinhos da Iria.

"Keep going to the Cova da Iria for the next two months, and pray the Rosary every day," she instructed.

In September the crowds were larger than before. People shouted their requests to the children as they walked. Lucia told Our Lady all their needs.

"Next month," Our Lady said, "there will be a miracle so that everyone may believe."

October 13 was a rainy day. Nonetheless, seventy thousand people came to the Cova da Iria in Fatima.

"Close your umbrellas!" Lucia called out, even though it was still raining. "Let's pray the Rosary!" Soon the children saw the flash of light, and Our Lady appeared.

"What do you want?" Lucia asked.

"I want a chapel built here in my honor. I am the Lady of the Rosary," the Blessed Mother answered. "This war will end soon. Pray the Rosary every day for peace and the conversion of sinners."

After speaking with the children, Our Lady opened her hands. Rays of light streamed from them as she began to rise up into the sky.

"Look at the sun!" Lucia shouted to the crowd.

Everyone looked up. The sun was spinning and different colors of light shot out from its edges like fireworks. Some feared the sun would crash to earth.

"Miracle! Miracle!" the people exclaimed as many fell to their knees.

The shepherds never saw the miracle of the sun. Instead, Lucia, Francisco, and Jacinta saw Saint Joseph and Jesus along with Mary. Jesus was blessing the world.

Suddenly, everything and everyone was completely dry.

Everything that the Blessed Mother had told the three shepherds turned out to be true. The war did end. Francisco and Jacinta went to heaven while they were still young. Lucia lived until she was ninety-eight years old. As a religious sister, Lucia continued to pray and brought Our Lady's message to the world.

Today, people from every nation visit Fatima in Portugal. They go to ask Our Lady of the Rosary to pray for them and the people they love. They also pray for peace and the conversion of sinners. But we don't have to go to Fatima to do what Our Lady asked. We can pray the Rosary every day, make small sacrifices to God, honor the Immaculate Heart of Mary, and live our lives with heaven in our hearts.

Prayers of Fatima

Pardon Prayer

My God, I believe, I adore, I hope, and I love you. And I ask pardon for those who do not believe, do not adore, do not hope, and do not love you.

Prayer to the Holy Trinity

Most Holy Trinity—Father, Son, and Holy Spirit—I adore you profoundly. I offer you the Most Precious Body, Blood, Soul, and Divinity of Jesus Christ, present in all the tabernacles of the world, in reparation for the outrages, sacrileges, and indifferences whereby he is offended. And through the infinite merits of his Most Sacred Heart and the Immaculate Heart of Mary, I beg of you the conversion of poor sinners.

Eucharistic Prayer

Most Holy Trinity, I adore you! My God, my God, I love you in the Most Blessed Sacrament.

Sacrifice Prayer

O my Jesus, I offer this for love of you, for the conversion of sinners, and in reparation for the sins committed against the Immaculate Heart of Mary.

Decade Prayer

O My Jesus, forgive us our sins, save us from the fires of hell, lead all souls to heaven, especially those in most need of your mercy.

Prayer asking the intercession of the Little Shepherds of Fatima

Dear Shepherds of Fatima,
How wonderful it must have been to see Mary, the Mother of God!
It took a lot of courage for you to be her messengers, especially when people refused to believe you, or made fun of you.
Thank you for bringing us Mary's important message about prayer and sacrifice.
Help me to pray for the peace that our world needs so badly.
Help me to offer my own acts of love and sacrifice to make up for the sins that offend God and the Blessed Mother.
Remind me that even though I am young, my love and my efforts to be like Jesus can make a real difference in the world.
Please pray for me. Amen.

How to Pray the Rosary

1. Make the sign of the cross and
   pray the Apostles' Creed.
2. Pray the Our Father.
3. Pray 3 Hail Marys.
4. Pray the Glory, name the first
   Mystery, and pray the Our Father.

5. Pray 10 Hail Marys.
6. Pray the Glory, name
   the second Mystery, and
   pray the Our Father.
7. Repeat steps 5 and 6
   until you reach the end.
8. Pray the Glory and
   the Hail, Holy Queen.
   Kiss the Crucifix.

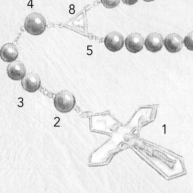

The Sign of the Cross

In the name of the Father, and of the Son, and of the Holy Spirit.
Amen.

The Apostles' Creed

I believe in God, the Father almighty,
creator of heaven and earth.
I believe in Jesus Christ, his only Son, our Lord.
He was conceived by the power of the Holy Spirit and born of the Virgin Mary.
He suffered under Pontius Pilate, was crucified, died, and was buried.
He descended to the dead.
On the third day he rose again.
He ascended into heaven, and is seated at the right hand of the Father.
He will come again to judge the living and the dead.
I believe in the Holy Spirit,
the holy catholic Church,
the communion of saints,
the forgiveness of sins,
the resurrection of the body,
and the life everlasting. Amen.

Our Father

Our Father, who art in heaven, hallowed be thy name. Thy kingdom come, thy will be done on earth as it is in heaven. Give us this day our daily bread, and forgive us our trespasses, as we forgive those who trespass against us. And lead us not into temptation, but deliver us from evil. Amen.

Hail Mary

Hail Mary, full of grace, the Lord is with thee. Blessed art thou among women, and blessed is the fruit of thy womb, Jesus. Holy Mary, Mother of God, pray for us sinners, now and at the hour of our death. Amen.

Glory Be

Glory be to the Father, and to the Son, and to the Holy Spirit: as it was in the beginning, is now, and ever shall be, world without end. Amen.

Fatima Decade Prayer

O My Jesus, forgive us our sins, save us from the fires of hell, lead all souls to heaven, especially those in most need of your mercy.

Hail, Holy Queen

Hail, holy Queen, Mother of Mercy, our life, our sweetness, and our hope. To thee do we cry, poor banished children of Eve; to thee do we send up our sighs, mourning, and weeping in this valley of tears. Turn then, most gracious advocate, thine eyes of mercy toward us, and after this our exile, show unto us the blessed fruit of thy womb, Jesus. O clement, O loving, O sweet Virgin Mary.

Closing Prayers

Pray for us, O holy Mother of God,
that we may be made worthy of the promises of Christ.

O God, whose Only-Begotten Son, by his life, death, and resurrection has purchased for us the rewards of eternal life, grant we beseech thee, that while meditating upon these mysteries of the most holy Rosary of the Blessed Virgin Mary, we may imitate what they contain and obtain what they promise, through the same Christ our Lord. Amen.

The Joyful Mysteries

We pray the Joyful Mysteries on Mondays and Saturdays.

1. The Annunciation of the Archangel Gabriel to Mary
2. The Visitation of Mary to Her Cousin Elizabeth
3. The Nativity
4. The Presentation in the Temple
5. The Finding of Jesus in the Temple

The Mysteries of Light

We pray the Mysteries of Light on Thursdays.

1. The Baptism of Jesus
2. The Wedding at Cana
3. Jesus Announces God's Kingdom
4. The Transfiguration
5. Jesus Gives Us the Holy Eucharist

The Sorrowful Mysteries

We pray the Sorrowful Mysteries on Tuesdays and Fridays.

1. The Agony in the Garden
2. The Scourging at the Pillar
3. The Crowning with Thorns
4. The Carrying of the Cross
5. The Crucifixion

The Glorious Mysteries

We pray the Glorious Mysteries on Wednesdays and Sundays.

1. The Resurrection
2. The Ascension
3. The Descent of the Holy Spirit
4. The Assumption
5. The Coronation

For Grown-ups

An apparition is a mystical vision that God sends for a purpose. This is not something new. The Bible records them in both the Old and New Testaments. And over the centuries numerous claims of apparitions have been investigated by the Church. Our Lady of the Rosary at Fatima is one of several apparitions of the Blessed Virgin Mary that have been approved.

At the height of World War I, in the spring of 1916, the Angel of Peace first appeared to Lucia dos Santos and her younger cousins, Francisco and Jacinta Marto. As a result of the angel's three visits, the children chose to deepen their prayer life, make sacrifices for the conversion of sinners, and console Jesus and Mary. The angel also taught them to adore Jesus in the Holy Eucharist. Then he actually gave them the Body and Blood of Christ. For the two youngest shepherds, seven-year-old Francisco and six-year-old Jacinta, it was their first Holy Communion!

Eight months after the angel's last visit, the Virgin Mary appeared to the three little shepherds. She stood on a holm oak tree at the Cova da Iria on May 13, 1917. The Blessed Mother returned to the same spot for the next six months except for August, when the children were prevented from meeting her there. During the July apparition, Mary revealed a secret in three parts. The children kept these to themselves. Much intrigue has surrounded this aspect of the apparitions at Fatima. By the year 2000, however, Lucia had revealed all three parts to the appropriate people at the appropriate times. One of the elements of the secret was the consecration of Russia to the Immaculate Heart of Mary and the promotion of the First Saturday Devotion.

Francisco and Jacinta Marto, who both died within three years of the last apparition, were beatified by Pope Saint John Paul II on May 13, 2000. Pope Francis canonized them on May 13, 2017. Sister Lucia, who had become a Discalced Carmelite nun, attended the beatification Mass. She was ninety-three years old. Sister Lucia died five years later on February 13, 2005. The cause for her beatification has been opened.

The message of Fatima was not just for the three shepherds, nor is its relevance limited to the twentieth century. The angel and the Virgin Mary invited Lucia, Francisco, and Jacinta into a deeper life of faith. They prayed the Rosary daily for peace, made sacrifices for the conversion of sinners, and honored the Immaculate Heart of Mary. The shepherds of Fatima inspire us—and Jesus and his mother, Mary, invite us—to do the same.